THE
KENT & EAST SUSSEX
RAILWAY

·A PAST and PRESENT COMPANION·

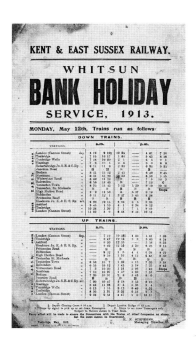

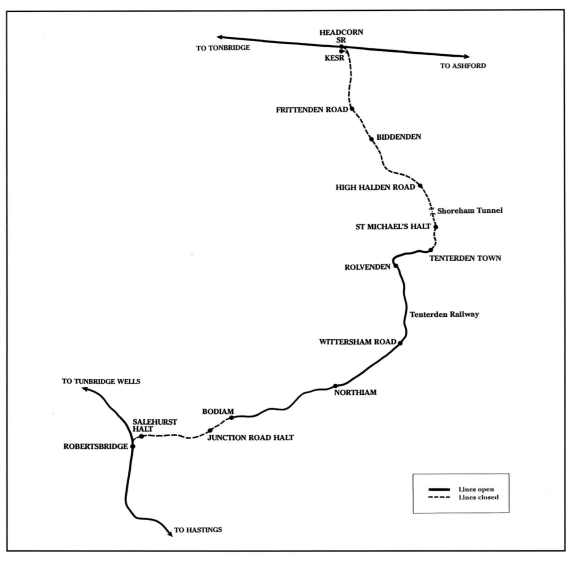

HEADCORN
SR

TO TONBRIDGE

KESR

TO ASHFORD

FRITTENDEN ROAD

BIDDENDEN

HIGH HALDEN ROAD

Shoreham Tunnel

ST MICHAEL'S HALT

TENTERDEN TOWN

ROLVENDEN

Tenterden Railway

WITTERSHAM ROAD

TO TUNBRIDGE WELLS

NORTHIAM

SALEHURST
HALT

BODIAM

ROBERTSBRIDGE

JUNCTION ROAD HALT

TO HASTINGS

Lines open
Lines closed

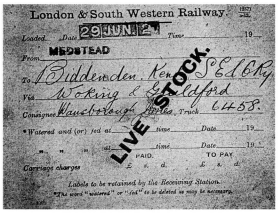

London & South Western Railway. (457)
Loaded. Date 29 JUN 2 Time 19
From MEDSTEAD
To Biddenden Ken SE&LCRy
Via Woking & Guildford
Consignee Wansborough Jones Truck 6458
*Watered and (or) fed at time Date 19
" " " at time Date 19
PAID. TO PAY.
Carriage charges £ s. d. £ s. d.
Labels to be retained by the Receiving Station.
*The word "watered" or "fed" to be deleted as may be necessary.

LIVE STOCK.

THE
KENT & EAST SUSSEX RAILWAY

· A PAST AND PRESENT COMPANION ·

A nostalgic journey along the whole route from Headcorn to Robertsbridge

Terry Gough

· RAILWAY HERITAGE ·
from
The NOSTALGIA Collection

First published in 1998
Reprinted 2004

British Library Cataloguing in Publication Data

A catalogue record for this book is available from the British Library.

ISBN 1 85895 149 6

Past & Present Publishing Ltd
The Trundle
Ringstead Road
Great Addington
Kettering
Northamptonshire NN14 4BW

Tel/Fax: 01536 330588
email: sales@nostalgiacollection.com
Website: www.nostalgiacollection.com

Map drawn by Christina Siviter

Printed and bound in Great Britain

Below right A KESR letter dated 5 July 1907: the 'bill' presumably refers to an advertisement for a special event, and the letter is signed by Colonel Stephens.

A Past & Present book
from
The NOSTALGIA *Collection*

ACKNOWLEDGEMENTS

I have been supported in the preparation of this book by the management of the Tenterden Railway Company, and wish to thank in particular Graham Hukins. I also thank Doug Lindsay, John Miller, Philip Shaw and Gerald Siviour, all of whom have given their time willingly. I am most grateful to the numerous photographers who have loaned me their material, without which it would not have been possible to produce this book; their names appear under the relevant photographs. Finally I thank my wife Cynthia who, having experienced one visit to the closed line in snow in 1958, has encouraged me to make all subsequent visits on my own!

To avoid ambiguity in the captions, I have used the abbreviation 'KESR' to refer to the line up to closure by BR, and 'Tenterden Railway' to refer to the line thereafter.

ABBREVIATIONS

BR	British Railways		LBSCR	London, Brighton & South Coast Railway
DMU	Diesel multiple unit		LNWR	London & North Western Railway
EMU	Electric multiple unit		LSWR	London & South Western Railway
GWR	Great Western Railway		SECR	South Eastern & Chatham Railway
KESR	Kent & East Sussex Railway		SR	Southern Railway

BIBLIOGRAPHY

Garrett, Stephen *The Kent and East Sussex Railway* (Oakwood Press, 1987)
Mitchell, Vic, and Smith, Keith *Branch Line to Tenterden* (Middleton Press, 1985)
Scott-Morgan, John *Railways of Arcadia* (P. E. Waters & Associates, 1989)

CONTENTS

Kent and East Sussex Railway.

Telephone:
28 TONBRIDGE.
Telegrams:
"STEPHENS, TONBRIDGE STATION."

MANAGING DIRECTOR'S OFFICE,

TONBRIDGE,

July 5th 19 07

Dear Sir,

Please have enclosed bill put up where it can be seen also try and sell the ticket enclosed and if you want any more I will send and get them for you.

Yours truly,

Mr. Dyers
Biddenden.

Rolvenden in December 1953, a few days before closure. Class 'O1' No 31065 completes its shunting operation, while Class 'A1X' No 32678, on a mixed train from Robertsbridge, waits for access to the station.

The same location in August 1995, with engine No 14 *Charwelton* and its rake of vintage coaches on an afternoon train from Northiam. Although an industrial engine, it is not out of place on the Tenterden Railway, as a very similar engine was used on the Weston, Clevedon & Portishead Light Railway, another Colonel Stephens railway. *Colin Hogg, courtesy of Mike Esau/TG*

INTRODUCTION

My own introduction to the KESR was on the first day of 1954, when I travelled by train from Chessington via Waterloo East to Headcorn. My knowledge of the KESR was negligible, but I recall being amazed at the sight of an ex-SECR Class 'O1' on a single-coach train, which left virtually empty. I do not remember seeing any passengers boarding at the intermediate stations, and I was surprised by the leisurely rate of progress of the train and the decrepit state of St Michael's Halt. I could not see the logic of running trains only as far as Tenterden Town, then expecting passengers to wait for ages before proceeding southward. The reasons for closure were, however, clear, and this took place the following day. I spent the day on the line, and managed to buy a 1st Class ticket at Tenterden, despite no 1st Class service being provided since the 1930s. I arrived at Robertsbridge at 5.30pm on the last train of the day, and caught a connecting train to London.

This early experience led me to visit the line on numerous occasions; I walked the length of it from Headcorn to Rolvenden twice in 1955, and in the next few years travelled on several special passenger trains on the southern section.

So what was the origin of this railway, which connected three small towns and managed to miss several villages en route? It was built as a Light Railway from the Robertsbridge end as far as the present-day Rolvenden, and was opened in 1900. In 1903 it was extended to Tenterden Town, necessitating a long climb at 1 in 50. The company changed its name from the Rother Valley Railway to the Kent & East Sussex Railway the following year, presumably to give its shareholders and the public an indication of a much larger network. Indeed, the line was extended northward to Headcorn in 1905, this section being much more substantially built than the southern end of the line. At both Robertsbridge and Headcorn the railway had interchange platforms with the SECR, the former on the London to Hastings line and the latter on the line from London to Ashford and beyond. The headquarters of the KESR were at Rolvenden, where there were engine and carriage sheds and a locomotive works. The KESR was one of several railways that Holman F. Stephens was instrumental in building or in which he otherwise had an interest. He managed all his railways from his head office in Tonbridge, only a few miles from Rolvenden.

The KESR was in effect run as two separate railways, with most trains starting either at Tenterden Town or Rolvenden. The heavier engines used on the northern section to Headcorn could not work south of Rolvenden, so an engine change was in any case necessary. No Sunday service was provided after the early years, other than on the southern section during the hop-picking season. In BR days there were five trains each way on the northern section and three at the Robertsbridge end, all of which were 3rd Class only.

The KESR was not included in the amalgamation of railway companies in 1923, when the SECR became part of the Eastern Section of the newly formed Southern Railway. It was always run as a basic railway with, for example, poor facilities for passengers at stations and ungated level crossings; some stations were served only on request. Much its rolling-stock and motive power was purchased second-hand from other railways, and it also borrowed engines from the SR on a regular basis. Despite this the line began to lose money in the 1920s and it is unlikely that it would have been any different had it become part of the SR.

There was a reasonable amount of freight traffic on the line and indirectly this may have led to a decline in passenger traffic. Most trains were mixed, which meant that passengers were kept waiting at intermediate stations while shunting was carried out. Attempts were made to address this and effect economies by introducing railbuses in the late 1920s, but none of this was sufficient to prevent the ever-increasing loss of traffic to road competition.

The KESR did lose its independence in 1948 and became part of the Southern Region of British Railways. It was not long before it was evident to the new owners that the line was unlikely ever to make money and it was decided to close it. All regular passenger services were withdrawn from Monday 4 January 1954; as there was no Sunday service, the last train ran on 2 January. The Headcorn to Tenterden Town section was closed completely, but the southern part of the line was kept open for freight and occasional passenger trains. The latter were for what are now referred to as 'special interest groups', in reality hop-pickers and their friends, ramblers and, of course, railway enthusiasts. All trains continued to be worked by Class 'A1X' tank engines, due to the severe weight restrictions on the numerous bridges. Diesel locomotives were introduced in 1957, although steam was still used occasionally. All workings ceased in 1961, except on the short section from Robertsbridge to the nearby mill, which became a private siding.

Most of the stations lay abandoned from the withdrawal of regular passenger services. On the southern section the halts at Salehurst and Junction Road and the stations at Wittersham Road and Rolvenden were demolished. The two remaining stations of Bodiam and Northiam on the southern half of the line were just left to deteriorate. Tenterden Town and all the northern section stations (except St Michael's Halt) were retained, and some were eventually bought from BR for domestic or other uses. All survive to this day.

Schemes to preserve the southern part of the line were proposed shortly after it closed completely, but nothing came to fruition until 1971 when the Tenterden Railway Company was formed. This company purchased the line between Tenterden Town and Bodiam and began the enormous task of rebuilding the infrastructure and acquiring suitable stock with which to run the railway. A major setback to preservation had been the destruction of the site at Rolvenden and, worse, the sale of the land once occupied by the engine shed, works and yard to the neighbouring timber company. Fortunately the Tenterden site was little changed and Tenterden Town thus became the headquarters of the new company. The task of reinstating Tenterden and redeveloping Rolvenden was begun.

Tremendous effort was required and it was a mark of the dedication of the company and the volunteers of the associated preservation society that the passenger service between Tenterden and Rolvenden was reinstated on 3 February 1974, only three years after formation of the company. Wittersham Road station was reconstructed and services extended to there from June 1978. The next objective was Hexden Bridge, which was reached in 1983. Beyond this the railway crossed the River Rother and entered East Sussex. It was 1 mile from there to Northiam, where services were reintroduced in 1990. The service to Bodiam was re-instated in the year 2000.

Beyond Bodiam there are significant impediments to the re-opening of the railway. Track has been removed for much of the way and land used for other purposes, and just outside Robertsbridge the course of the line is cut by a new section of the A21 main road. Despite all this, a separate group called the Rother Valley Railway Company has plans for rebuilding this part of the line.

What has been achieved to rejuvenate the old KESR is remarkable and has exceeded the expectations of many people. Here is a railway that, with its beautifully turned-out locomotives and rolling-stock and smart stations, surpasses the achievements of the original railway, at least in these respects. The old and new have one important attribute in common, and that is the dedication of their employees to the provision of services to the public under severe financial constraints. The present-day railway has the great advantage that it also has the support of volunteers and opportunities for fund-raising and grant applications, inappropriate to the KESR in the earlier part of this century. It is a pleasure to visit the new railway over 40 years since I first encountered the old KESR.

Terry Gough
Sherborne, Dorset

Headcorn

On 5 April 1958 'West Country' Class No 34104 *Bere Alston*, masking its train, the 11.02am Ramsgate to Charing Cross, passes Headcorn on the up through line. The remnant of the KESR line, which curves away to the right, was used for the storage of condemned rolling-stock. The unseasonal spring snowfall had caught the cyclists (including the author and his future wife) by surprise, and they are returning to London prematurely by the next stopping train.

What a contrast! Headcorn is no longer a junction and the course of the KESR line is buried in undergrowth. An up relief line for freight trains, behind the metal fence, passes over the site of the KESR platform. The main line has been electrified and as well as services to and from the Kent Coast, Eurostar trains pass through Headcorn. This is the 17.22 Brussels Midi to Waterloo train on 4 August 1995. *Both TG*

Four views of the KESR Headcorn station. The first shows a typical KESR train in BR days, with Class 'O1' No 31065, a 'birdcage' passenger brake-van and a few wagons. The main line is to the right. The KESR referred to the station as Headcorn Junction, but to the SECR and its successors it was plain Headcorn. The same applied at Robertsbridge.

The second view shows the basic facilities provided for KESR passengers. Class 'O1' No 31370 heads a Tenterden Town train in April 1951.

A visit almost exactly two years after closure revealed that the platform road had been removed, but otherwise little had changed.

Remnants of the platform can still be found in the undergrowth and the course of the line in the vicinity of the station is recognisable. There is still a footbridge across the main line, which gives access to the site of the KESR platform, although it has been replaced and resited. *Neil Sprinks/A. J. Pike, courtesy of Frank Hornby/TG (2)*

11

Kent and East Sussex Railway.

NOT AVAILABLE when this

Excess Fare Receipt №. 9055

Corner is
cut off at
end of
Journey

Issued at.......................

Date................ Train.........

Excessed from ....

to.............................

		Single	Return	Fare	£	s.	d.
......Class without Ticket							
......(Class travelled on No. of Ticket held ....)							
3rd Class to 1st							
Excess Luggage, weight. ...lbs.							
Dogs accompanied by passenger							
Bicycles ,, ,,							
Prams							
Folding Prams							
	TOTAL ...						

Collector.....................

TO BE SHOWN OR GIVEN UP ON DEMAND

Issued subject to Conditions shown in Public Notices and Time Books
Available on day of issue and train stated only.

An uncharacteristically long mixed train has just arrived from Rolvenden. The poor state of the sleepers gives an indication of the severe financial problems that faced the KESR, both as an independent railway and subsequent to its absorption by BR. Despite this, some of the line was relaid in BR days, not long before closure!

The second view shows the abandoned station, with the waiting shelter and some of the track removed, in the mid-1950s.

The only visible items to link this 1996 photograph with the past are the main-line platforms and the trees in the right background. *Lens of Sutton (2)/TG*

This really is the end of the line: track lifting is in progress between Headcorn and Frittenden Road in November 1955.

Today the land is flat in this area and the course of the line is not easy to find, other than at former level crossings or where the railway was bordered by hedges. This is one such location in 1996, as near as can be judged to the past location. *Both TG*

KESR ticket 0040 in the style of contemporary SR tickets.

Frittenden Road

The road entrance to Frittenden Road station on 11 August 1987, long after it had been abandoned. The building behind the station may have been erected during the Second World War, at the same time as similar buildings at Tenterden Town (see page 33).

Today there is life again at Frittenden Road and the old station yard is used for the sale of second-hand cars and building materials. Both the station buildings and the adjacent corrugated-roofed building still stand, although the former is in a very poor state of repair. *Both TG*

KESR engine No 4 is ready to leave Frittenden Road on a Tenterden Town train in 1933. No 4 was an ex-LSWR engine of Class '330', obtained from the SR in 1932 as No 0335. The coach was also of LSWR origin and provided five 3rd Class compartments. At Frittenden Road, in common with several other stations, a single post sufficed for signalling in both directions. The signals were provided to indicate whether there were any intending passengers, as this was a request stop. The railway crossed a minor road at this point, which led to the village of Frittenden 2 miles away. A more direct road ran from the village to Headcorn, a distance of under 3 miles. It is therefore not surprising that this was one of the quietest stations on the KESR.

On 13 November 1955 Frittenden Road station's canopy was already developing an unhealthy sag, and the building was allowed to decay slowly over many years.

By 1995 the canopy had virtually collapsed and it was not possible to approach the station along the trackbed. *Lens of Sutton/TG (2)*

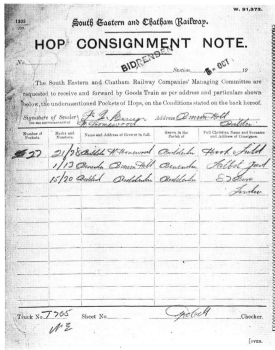

Right A hop consignment note. The transport of hops was a major source of income for the KESR throughout its existence, and most stations dispatched them.

Biddenden

Class 'O1' No 31065 storms into Biddenden on a mixed train on the last day of services in January 1954.

By contrast, on an earlier occasion another member of the class, No 31064, drifts into the station with a single-coach train.

The station and yard are now in private ownership. The trackbed lies immediately beyond the two white posts and runs left to right, this being the nearest alignment to the past location, without showing nothing more than trees. *D. Trevor Rowe, courtesy of The Colonel Stephens Railway Museum/Lens of Sutton/TG*

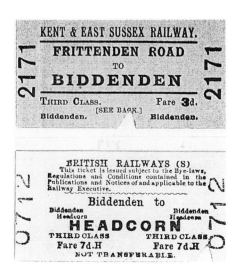

A winter view in BR days with No 31065 on a Tenterden Town train at Biddenden. The ungated crossing over the Headcorn to Biddenden road is behind the camera. Biddenden was provided with electric light, a luxury many larger stations on the Southern Region did not have.

The second photograph is looking north at the abandoned station in the winter of 1955. Biddenden was the only station north of Tenterden Town to have a passing loop, with up and down platforms.

Both platforms still exist, at least in part. The station canopy has been replaced by a brick built-extension to the original building, much of which still stands and at the time of the visit (1995) was undergoing renovation. *Lens of Sutton/TG (2)*

KENT & EAST SUSSEX RAILWAY

On and after

Saturday Mar. 6, 1915,

and every Saturday until further notice,

Passengers per the 9.55 a.m. up train ex Headcorn, Biddenden 10.7 a.m., Tenterden 10.25 a.m., and Northiam 10.45 a.m. will reach

TUNBRIDGE WELLS 1.16 p.m.,

Tonbridge 1.27 p.m.,

LONDON, (CHARING CROSS,) 2.42 P.M.,

Maidstone 2.56 p.m.,

owing to the withdrawal of connecting train by S. E. & C. R. Co. On other weekdays the connection is as shown on October Timetables.

TONBRIDGE,
March 1st, 1915.

H. F. STEPHENS,
Managing Director.

A72679

Printed at the Company's Works, Rolvenden.

Left According to this notice of 6 March 1915, Maidstone-bound passengers were expected to travel south on the KESR, change to the SECR at Robertsbridge, then change again at Tonbridge, involving a journey time of 5 hours and a distance of 49 miles. The KESR neglected to mention that by joining an SECR train at Headcorn, the journey time to Maidstone was only 2 hours, a distance of 20 miles.

Class 'O1' No 31064 heads a demolition train loaded with recently lifted rails at Biddenden in the summer of 1955. The station has only been closed for about 18 months, but already the track is disappearing beneath the undergrowth, which is also encroaching on to the platforms. Engines almost always worked chimney-first from Headcorn throughout the life of the line, but this tradition was broken during demolition.

The trackbed has been cleared at this point, although the platform faces are hidden by bushes in this 1995 view. The Headcorn to Biddenden village road is at the end of this lane. *Lens of Sutton/TG*

High Halden Road

This 1952 view of the station, looking toward Tenterden Town, shows the overgrown and empty goods yard.
The station building still stands, but the trackbed has disappeared beneath weeds and bushes. This summer 1996 view is from a slightly different angle, necessitated by the erection of buildings on the site of the goods yard.
H. C. Casserley/TG

Looking toward Headcorn from the level crossing at High Halden Road in BR days finds No 31065 on a mixed train. The double-arm 'request stop' signal was the last to survive on the line, and was redundant, as High Halden Road had become a compulsory stop even before BR took over the KESR. The Frittenden Road and Biddenden signals had been removed some years previously, despite the fact that Frittenden Road remained a request stop right up to closure.

A visit shortly after track lifting in 1955 found the station deserted, but otherwise in fairly good condition, with no broken windows or other products of vandalism.

The land later passed into private ownership and was used for several years for a market garden business, as seen here on 11 August 1987. The station yard is currently derelict and awaiting sale. *Lens of Sutton/TG (2)*

On the last day of passenger services (2 January 1954), the 10.55am from Headcorn to Tenterden Town was strengthened to two coaches. It is seen here hauled by No 31065, leaving High Halden Road with plenty of interest being shown in the photographer, at least from the first coach. The author had travelled on this train the previous day, when there were very few other passengers.

It is easy to recognise the 'past' location today, with the course of the railway running behind the now untrimmed hedge. This is the view on 24 September 1996. *Colin Hogg, courtesy of Mike Esau/TG*

Shoreham Tunnel

About 1 mile south of High Halden Road the railway entered a short tunnel, known as Shoreham Tunnel. This photograph of the north portal, taken about 1925, shows the track free of weeds and a clear embankment.

In contrast, this photograph taken in November 1955, only two years after closure, gives an indication of how the railway had become overgrown.

The tunnel still exists and this June 1996 photograph shows the cutting surprisingly clear of obstructions. There has been much housing development in the area around the tunnel, although the houses in the immediate vicinity are hidden by trees. *The Colonel Stephens Railway Museum/TG (2)*

St Michael's Halt

There was a short cutting beyond the south end of the tunnel, after which the line crossed a minor road and passed over more open land. At the road crossing, which was ungated, a halt was erected in 1912 to serve the local community of St Michael's. This is the halt in both a dangerous and decrepit condition only eight months after the end of passenger services. The road crossing is behind the camera.

The old line is now used as a foot and cycle path, as this 1996 view shows. *Both TG*

This photograph, taken a few years before closure, shows the halt in slightly better condition. The road crossing is in the background and the beginning of the cutting can be seen beyond this.

The location is unrecognisable when viewed from the same place, as the cottages in the 'past' photograph are hidden behind the trees. The level crossing was situated between the two cars. It is not possible to continue over the crossing toward the tunnel mouth, as bungalows now occupy the area. *Lens of Sutton/TG*

Above This scene typifies the KESR, with an engine (Class 'O1' No 31370) almost as long as its train, pushing its way through the undergrowth. The location is between St Michael's Halt and Tenterden Town and the date is 12 September 1953. *Colin Hogg, courtesy of Mike Esau*

Below Much of the KESR was bounded on both sides by fields with frequent crossings for cattle or vehicles. Many of the gates had brass plates attached, such as seen here. *TG*

Tenterden Town

This was the end of the line just beyond Tenterden Town in 1955, after the dismantling of the northern section.
    The present end of the line is a few yards short of the 'past' end. Beyond here the course of the railway disappears into thick wood before reaching the footpath shown on pages 28 and 29. The coach is one of a small number designed for the SECR for boat train use and had unusual 'matchboard' body panels. *Both TG*

Engine No 31065 was regularly used on the KESR and is seen here just south of the present end of the line, on the 11.35am Tenterden Town to Headcorn train on 28 December 1953. This engine was withdrawn by BR in 1961 and went to the Ashford Steam Centre. Following closure of the centre in the 1980s, it was privately stored until transfer to the Bluebell Railway in 1997.

    The stretch of line now forms part of the head shunt for Tenterden Town and thus still sees occasional trains.
Colin Hogg, courtesy of Mike Esau/TG

This general view of Tenterden Town station and goods yard on 13 November 1955 shows considerable traffic, despite closure north of here. The triangular construction in the centre background is a wind pump, used to supply water to the tower at the other end of the station. The corrugated-roofed buildings on the extreme right were erected during the Second World War for the storage of food.

A visit in June 1996 finds an even more active yard, this time predominantly passenger stock, including Pullman cars, which are used on the 'Wealden Pullman' wine-and-dine trains. The diesel shunter is ex-BR Class '03' No D2023, which arrived on the Tenterden Railway in 1983. It currently carries the number 46. *Both TG*

This pre-Nationalisation photograph of Tenterden Town station is looking towards Rolvenden, showing the little-used island platform on the right-hand side.

The second view shows an uncharacteristically long train at Tenterden Town on 18 October 1959, almost six years after withdrawal of regular passenger services. This is a ramblers' excursion that had originated from Victoria; at Robertsbridge one 'Terrier' was attached to each end of the train for its journey to Tenterden and back. The engine in the foreground is Class 'A1' No DS680. This was LBSCR No 54, which was sold to the SECR in 1904. It was renumbered 680s in 1932 and was used for pilot duties at Lancing Carriage Works until 1962.

The site of the island platform is now occupied by carriage sidings and a carriage workshop. The coach in Pullman livery on the extreme left is a BR Mark 1 restaurant car, which has been given the name 'Diana' by the Tenterden Railway Company. *Lens of Sutton/TG (2)*

KENT & EAST SUSSEX RAILWAY.
Issued subject to the Bye-laws, Regulations & Conditions in the Company's Bills and Notices.
Tenterden to
0193

Via _____ & Southern Rly.
First Class. Fare — /-
NOT TRANSFERABLE.
0193

KENT & EAST SUSSEX RAILWAY.
TENTERDEN TOWN
TO
ROBERTSBRIDGE JUNCTION
2192
FIRST CLASS. Fare 2/-
[SEE BACK.]
Robertsb'ge Jct.   Robertsb'ge Jct

The upper SR-style KESR ticket was issued to the author on the penultimate day of passenger services for use in non-existent 1st Class accommodation.

The few passengers are at least interested in the train! This pre-Nationalisation photograph shows Class 'A1X' No 2640 at Tenterden Town after hauling an ex-LSWR corridor coach and SR goods brake-van from Robertsbridge. It may well have started out with a few goods wagons that have been left at intermediate stations. The engine later became BR No 32640 and ended its working life under BR on the Hayling Island branch with other 'Terriers' that had been used on the KESR. It was sold to Butlins in 1964 and is now on the Isle of Wight Steam Railway.

On 5 June 1996 ex-GWR Class '1600' pannier tank No 1638 enters Tenterden Town. The signal box was obtained by the Tenterden Railway Company from BR at Chilham in 1973. *Lens of Sutton/TG*

Another 'Terrier', No 32678, is seen at Tenterden Town on a freight train from Robertsbridge a few years after withdrawal of passenger services. This engine is now owned by the Tenterden Railway Company.

No 32650 and its train in 1996 provide almost a mirror image of the 'past' photograph, even to the station canopy. Following withdrawal from service by BR, this engine was moved to the KESR in 1964 and hauled the first train on the re-opened railway on 3 February 1974. The engine is owned by the London Borough of Sutton and carried the name of the town until it was repainted in BR lined black livery. *David Lawrence, courtesy of Hugh Davies/TG*

KESR engine No 4 stands with a Robertsbridge train at Tenterden Town. Although undated, the photograph must be before 1938 as after that date the engine received a different boiler that hid the safety valves.

The second photograph is another view of the special train from Victoria at Tenterden Town on 18 October 1959. Class 'A1X' No 32670 was bought by the Rother Valley Railway from the LBSCR as Class 'A1' No 70 in 1901, when it became No 3 *Bodiam*. It was converted to Class 'A1X' in 1943, was taken over by BR in 1948 and became No 32670. It continued to work on the KESR until closure, and was purchased in 1964 for eventual use on the Tenterden Railway and again became No 3 *Bodiam*. It is currently awaiting restoration. Of necessity all the coaches are of the special narrow-bodied Restriction '0' type built for the Hastings line, including the Pullman car second from the front. An identical vehicle has been preserved by the Tenterden Railway Company.

There are five standard War Department Austerity 0-6-0 saddle tanks on the Tenterden Railway. During 1985 No 23 *Holman F. Stephens* was painted in camouflage green and reverted to its original number of WD 191. It is seen at Tenterden Town on 11 August 1987 on a train for Wittersham Road, the then southern terminus of the re-opened line. *Lens of Sutton/TG (2)*

Class 'O1' No 31048 rests at Tenterden Town after the exertion of bringing its one-coach train from Headcorn in the early 1950s. Like the other members of its class based at Ashford, its other duties included pilot at the Carriage & Wagon Works there. It was also to be seen in other parts of Kent and sometimes worked the Tilmanstone coal trains on the former East Kent Railway, which had also belonged to Colonel Stephens. It was withdrawn from service in 1960 and cut up.

The substantial changes that have taken place at Tenterden Town are reflected in this 'present' view from the site of the old island platform. What has not changed is the concrete lamp posts, to the right of the engine in both photographs. No 14 *Charwelton* is at the head of a train of vintage coaches on 5 June 1996. The first coach is a six-wheeled LNWR inspection saloon, which was used by the Longmoor Military Railway for many years. It arrived on the Tenterden Railway in 1985. *L. N. Owen, courtesy of Doug Lindsay/TG*

On towards Rolvenden

Just under a mile from Tenterden Town the line crossed the Cranbrook road. On 2 January 1954 Class 'A1X' No 32655 is climbing Tenterden bank at this point on the 12.20pm from Robertsbridge. This engine had the honour of working the last regular passenger train on the KESR later the same day. After withdrawal by BR in 1960 it went to the Bluebell Railway, where it can still be seen.

Large trees now dominate the location, which still gives good views of trains climbing the bank. Gates have been installed to protect the crossing; out of the peak season the box controlling the gates is not manned and the gates are operated by the train guard. All trains therefore stop here, as seen on 18 September 1996. *Colin Hogg, courtesy of Mike Esau/TG*

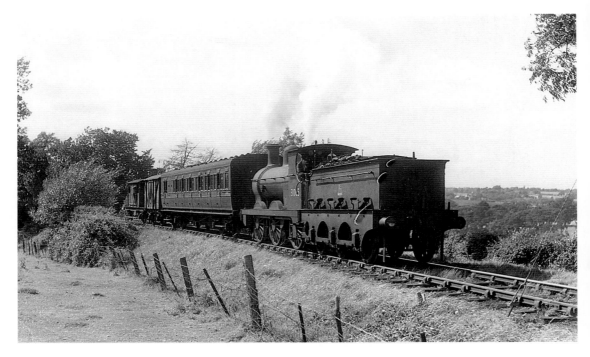

No 31065 ascends Tenterden bank on a mixed train from Rolvenden to Headcorn in early BR days. In the 'present' view ex-GWR pannier tank No 1636 in BR livery climbs past the same spot with its train of BR Mark 1 coaches on 5 August 1995. *Lens of Sutton/TG*

No 31065 is seen again, this time descending the bank with the 12.30pm Headcorn to Rolvenden train on the last day of BR services. Likewise No 1638 appears again in the 'present' photograph, this time in GWR livery, on an afternoon train from Tenterden Town to Northiam on 24 September 1996. *Colin Hogg, courtesy of Mike Esau/TG*

Earlier on the last day No 31065 worked the 9.35am Rolvenden to Headcorn train and has just passed the 10mph speed restriction near the bottom of Tenterden bank. Pannier tank No 1638 passes the same point nearly 43 years later; the rail-built signal is the outer home for Rolvenden. *Colin Hogg, courtesy of Mike Esau/TG*

Two 'Terriers' charge the bank on a special train on 19 October 1958. This is the 'Rother Valley Limited', which began its journey at Paddington. After visiting the KESR, it continued south to Bexhill West, then to Newhaven and finally to Victoria. The leading engine is No DS 377, the Brighton Works shunter from 1946 to 1959, which was painted in Stroudley livery. This was originally LBSCR No 35, and was withdrawn by BR in 1963 as No 32635. The rolling-stock for the KESR section of the trip consists of push-pull set No 723 (ex-LBSCR) and three non-corridor 3rd Class coaches of SECR origin.

The present Tenterden Railway vintage train, worked by No 14 *Charwelton*, tackles the bank on 5 August 1995. The coaches are ex-District Railway No 100, ex-Great Eastern Railway No 197 and ex-SECR family saloon, SR No 7913. No 100 had been used as a storage shed since 1902 and after a total rebuild entered service in 1984. No 197 (a six-wheeled Luggage Brake 3rd) had been used as a holiday home for many years before being acquired by the Tenterden Railway in the 1970s; it entered service in 1991. The huge amount of work involved in rebuilding these two coaches exemplifies both the dedication and the skill of those involved in the railway. No 7913 was sold by the SR to the Longmoor Military Railway in 1936. It did not need to be completely rebuilt, but there was still a great deal of work to be done before it entered service on the Tenterden Railway in 1993. *Both TG*

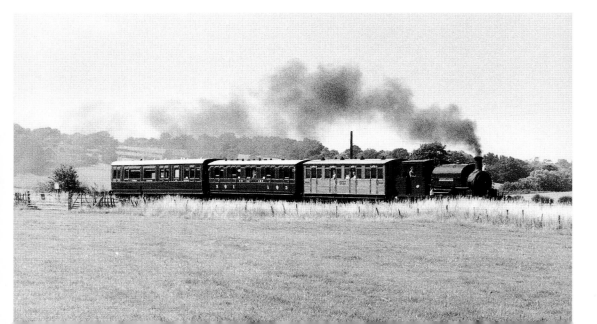

KESR engine No 8 is at the bottom of Tenterden bank with a train from Tenterden Town. Although undated, the photograph was probably taken between 1935 and 1937, as prior to 1935 No 8 displayed the name *Hesperus* and after 1937 was rarely used, being scrapped in 1941. The coach is ex-LSWR five-compartment Brake 3rd, SR No 2640, acquired in 1932 and broken up in 1948.

The second view shows the return 'Rother Valley Limited' with No 32678 at the front. The first coach, No 1110, is an SECR-designed ten-compartment 3rd. Vehicles of this type can be seen on the Bluebell Railway.

On 4 August 1995 No 14 *Charwelton* brings its train gently round the curve at the bottom of Tenterden bank, on which there is a 10mph speed restriction. The leading coach is again of SECR origin. *Lens of Sutton/TG (2)*

Ticket 0096 was used in conjunction with the 'Kent & East Sussex' special from London on 18 October 1959.

Another view of No 31064 in BR days with an ex-LSWR Brake 3rd coach and an SR goods brake-van, this time approaching the main road crossing at Rolvenden.

There are now two lines here, one being a siding on which are stored several locomotives awaiting restoration. The engine in the front without cab and boiler is No 12, an 0-4-0 industrial tank engine. Immediately behind is a diesel-electric built in 1932 for the Ford Motor Company and now numbered 40. Other engines in the line include the dismantled Class 'A1X' No 32670, three diesels (Nos 42, 47 and 506) and an Austerity saddle tank. No 47 is ex-BR Class '03' No D2024 and No 506 is Class '14' No D9504. *Lens of Sutton/TG*

Rolvenden

The 'Rother Valley Limited' of 19 October 1958 is taking water at the site of Rolvenden station, which had been demolished following withdrawal of passenger services. The crowds on the left are standing on what remains of the platform, and those on the right where the engine shed and workshop once stood.

The same location on 5 June 1996 shows dramatic changes, with the rebuilt station and a modern office building on the site of the engine shed. The new engine shed is located on the same side of the line as the station. *Both TG*

The signalman opens the gates over the A28 main road after the passage of the 11.15am Robertsbridge to Tenterden Town train, hauled by engine No 4 on 19 August 1933.

In the second photograph No 31065 runs light towards Tenterden Town on the penultimate day of passenger services in 1954.

The revitalised railway is exemplified by the smartly turned-out train, relaid track and new level crossing gates. This is the vintage train again, heading for Northiam on 4 August 1995. The barn on the left still exists, although almost completely hidden by trees. *H. C. Casserley/TG (2)*

A BR child single ticket issued on the penultimate day and erroneously dated 1 January 1955, and a BR-style Rolvenden platform ticket issued on 11 August 1987.

The two circa 1950 photographs show Class 'A1X' No 2644 at Rolvenden, and the view looking south, showing the engine shed on the right-hand side.

In the third view the 'Kent and East Sussex' special is seen at Rolvenden on 18 October 1959, with Class 'A1' No DS 680. Almost all that remains are the watering facilities.

The water tower features again in the August 1987 photograph. Since then there has been further significant change, the most obvious being the erection of a signal box on the right-hand side (see pages 63 and 64). *Lens of Sutton/The Colonel Stephens Railway Museum/TG (2)*

Two early photographs show No 4 arriving at Rolvenden on an empty carriage working on 19 August 1933, and railcar No 3 leaving Rolvenden for Robertsbridge. The latter unit was built by Shefflex Motors with bodywork added by a local company. It began work on the KESR in 1930 and was only used for about 10 years; it was scrapped after being stored for two years. The wagon on the rear is for passengers' baggage.

Everything not required by BR to run the freight-only service was demolished, as seen in the third view. The engine shed was on the left and the station on the other side.

However, Rolvenden has returned to life, with a new station and engine shed on the right-hand side, the site of the original shed no longer being owned by the railway. Two Austerity engines, No 24 *William H. Austen* and No 23 *Holman F. Stephens*, wait for duty. No 24 (ex-WD 200) arrived on the Tenterden Railway in 1971, and No 23 in 1972. *H. C. Casserley/Lens of Sutton (2)/TG*

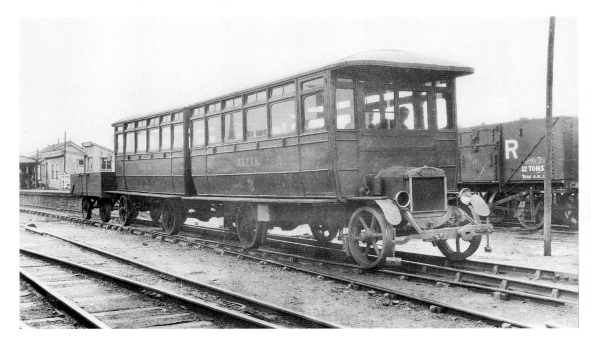

Class 'A1X' No 3 stands at Rolvenden with coach No 1 (ex-SR No 3121) forming the 9.48am to Robertsbridge on 26 April 1947.

The second photograph shows ex-LSWR Class '0395' engine, BR No 30576, at the same location; it was on loan to the KESR between 1940 and 1949. Few of this once numerous class passed into BR hands on Nationalisation, and none has been preserved.

The third view dates from 1967, in the early days of preservation, with Pullman car 'Barbara' in the through road at Rolvenden. This is one of several narrow-bodied vehicles built for the Hastings line, later to be downgraded to buffet cars. This vehicle was withdrawn by BR in 1963 and delivered to Robertsbridge the following year. It has since been restored to full Pullman condition and is used in the 'Wealden Pullman'

A present-day train hauled by pannier tank No 1638 enters the new station built by the Tenterden Railway Company. Features include an elevated viewing platform to enable visitors to see into the shed and yard. *H. C. Casserley/Lens of Sutton/TG (2)*

Outside the shed in this general view of Rolvenden from the south end of the site on 21 September 1935 is No 4. The building on the extreme left is the paint shop.

By 1957 the site is cleared of almost all buildings, as a short freight train hauled by Class 'A1X' No 32670 passes through.

By the 1970s there is the beginning of new life at Rolvenden, with two Class 'A1Xs'; the one in front, which is unmarked, became No 10 *Sutton* (ex-BR No 32650), while No 3 behind carries the name *Bodiam* (ex-BR No 32670). The railcar is ex-GWR No 20, which formed the first passenger train on the re-opening of the railway in February 1974.

An engine shed has now been built on this site and this is the view on 5 June 1996. From left to right, the engines at the front are Class '08' diesel shunter No 08108 (D3174), No 14 *Charwelton*, and Class '1600' No 1638.
H. C. Casserley/N. C. Simmons, courtesy of Hugh Davies/TG (2)

Another special train ran from London to Tenterden on 11 June 1961; this is the 'South Eastern Limited' on its return journey to Robertsbridge at Rolvenden. The train had earlier visited the Hawkhurst branch, which had closed to regular passenger traffic the previous day.

The same location on 5 June 1996 finds diesel shunter No 41 marshalling a goods train. The front brake-van is of standard SR design, and that on the rear is a six-wheeled SECR example. *Both TG*

As time went on Rolvenden yard became increasingly occupied by locomotives awaiting repair or scrap, most of which remained there until sold to raise money in the 1940s. In the front is No 1 *Tenterden*, bought by the Rother Valley Railway for the opening of its line; it was scrapped in 1941. On the left is Class 'A1X' No 5 *Rolvenden* (ex-LBSCR No 71), which was scrapped in 1939. The photograph was probably taken in the late 1930s.

Much of the area occupied by the yard is now owned by a sawmill, which bought the land to expand its own business, which was adjacent to the railway. *Lens of Sutton/TG*

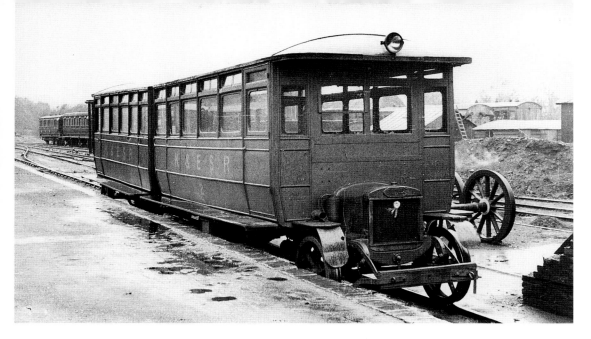

Here is the Shefflex-built railcar again, this time carrying the number 2, which it was given later in life (see page 54).

This 'present' photograph was taken a few yards further forward, as the exact location is occupied by oil storage tanks. The transformation that has taken place over the last few years is amazing; the railway looks vibrant and there is an air of activity and purpose. The steam engine is ex-SR Class 'USA' No DS 238 (formerly BR No 30070), and behind is diesel shunter No 08108. The former is one of two 'USA' tanks on the Tenterden Railway, both of which arrived in 1968. DS 238 was initially given the number 21 and named *Wainwright*, but has since reverted to its former BR departmental stock number. *Lens of Sutton/TG*

No 31065 shunts stock at the south end of Rolvenden in preparation to work the 3.15pm to Headcorn on 2 January 1954.

Austerity No 23 *Holman F. Stephens*, on a Tenterden-bound train, waits outside the station for a train to Northiam to pass on 4 August 1995. *Colin Hogg, courtesy of Mike Esau/TG*

Class 'A1X' No 32678 arrives at Rolvenden on the 12.20pm mixed train from Robertsbridge on 28 December 1953.
Class '14' diesel No D9525, built at Swindon in 1965, runs light into Rolvenden. Although a more substantial fence has been erected to the left of the railway, that on the right is little different to the one in the 'past' photograph. *Colin Hogg, courtesy of Mike Esau/TG*

Wittersham Road

With only another five weeks before the end of passenger services, Class 'A1X' No 32678 leaves Wittersham Road with the 12.20pm Robertsbridge to Tenterden mixed train.

After closure the station was demolished. As part of the rebuilding programme by the Tenterden Railway Company, the new platform was built to the right of the original in order to incorporate a passing loop. Austerity No WD191 (No 23) is waiting for the all clear to take its train of BR Mark 1 stock to Tenterden Town in the summer of 1987. At this time services only ran as far as Wittersham Road. Ex-GWR railcar No 20 had been moved from Rolvenden (see page 59) and unfortunately has suffered considerable decay. It is currently stored at Tenterden awaiting a rebuild. *Gerald Siviour/TG*

This undated photograph of Wittersham Road station shows the unusual position of the station building at right angles to the platform. The crossing is gated and the 'request stop' signals are in place. The photograph overleaf show the gates still in place in 1948, but the signals removed.

The new station building, which was obtained from BR at Borth, has been placed on the site of the original building. The signal box came from Dover and was rebuilt on this site in 1978. On 11 August 1987 No WD191 passes the signal box light as it runs round its train.
Lens of Sutton/TG

Wittersham Road station is seen here from the Robertsbridge end in 1948. According to the timetable the station was a compulsory stop for all trains from at least 1929 and possibly earlier.

The 'present' view shows the new station and signal box on 6 June 1996, with No 14 *Charwelton* on the last train of the day to Northiam. On the extreme left is the road entrance to the goods yard, which is now used by the Tenterden Railway's engineers department. The minor road in the foreground connects Rolvenden with Wittersham village, which is 2¼ miles south-east of the station. *The Colonel Stephens Railway Museum/TG*

Northiam

Here is another photograph of the 'Rother Valley Limited' in October 1958, this time at Northiam en route to Tenterden Town. The train was scheduled to stop for approximately 5 minutes at all stations on the KESR on its outward journey, but a glance at this photograph shows how impractical this was, with so many people (including the author) travelling on the train and wanting to record the event.

Unlike Wittersham Road, the station at Northiam was not demolished following closure to passenger services, so restoration was more straightforward. There was still significant expense, however – for example in the installation of level crossing gates over the A28 main road. No 14 *Charwelton* runs round its vintage coaches on 5 June 1996. *Both TG*

No 4 was photographed at Northiam on 10 August 1933, on a Tenterden Town train consisting of an ex-LSWR coach that had only recently arrived on the KESR. It survived until 1948.

The 'Kent and East Sussex' special also paused at Northiam on 18 October 1959, and is seen here with Class 'A1' No DS 680 at the head.

Northiam now regularly sees as many passengers at weekends as were brought by the specials of the late 1950s. This photograph, taken in June 1996, shows that it is much quieter during the week, at least until the summer holiday period. Pannier tank No 1638 waits to leave on the 11.50 to Tenterden Town. *H. C. Casserley/TG (2)*

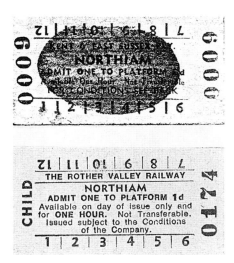

A mock SECR-style platform ticket issued by the Tenterden Railway Company in the 1980s, and a mock Rother Valley Railway ticket admitting one child to the platform. These tickets cannot be called replicas, because as far as can be established stations on the KESR did not issue platform tickets.

No 32678 shunts at Northiam in the late 1950s. The platform on the right had been removed many years earlier, but the passing loop has been retained.

By the summer of 1996 most of the work of restoring the second platform was complete, although it is not proposed to use this until trains are running through to Bodiam. An entrance to this platform direct from the main road is also in the course of construction. *David Lawrence, courtesy of Hugh Davies/TG*

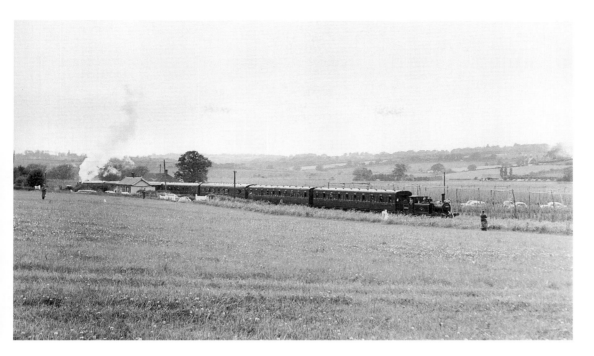

Bodiam

A special train in typical Kentish countryside, with hopfields in the background – except that this is East Sussex! The train has just left Bodiam on its way to Tenterden Town in the summer of 1961. The cars in the left and right background are on the B road that crosses the railway by Bodiam station. Bodiam Castle lies to the right, just out of view.

When this photograph was taken in the summer of 1996, a train service had not yet been re-instated, but the railway is in evidence with the track and Bodiam station still in place. There was only one platform at Bodiam and no provision for trains to pass. *Both TG*

This 6 August 1956 view of Bodiam is looking towards Rolvenden. At that time there were no level crossing gates, but it is believed that there were gates until about 1910.

Little has changed, as this 1996 view shows, other than the installation of level crossing gates. The station was waiting for the day when train services would be re-instated. *Hugh Davies/TG*

KENT & EAST SUSSEX RAILWAY.

1365

BODIAM
TO
WITTERSHAM Rd

Fare 6d.

THIRD CLASS.   [SEE BACK]   Witt. Rd.

Witt. Rd.

1365

Kent & East Sussex Railway

1561

BODIAM to
SALEHURST
Fare 5½d

THIRD CLASS   (See back)

A hop-pickers' special ready to leave Bodiam on a return trip to Robertsbridge in the late 1950s. Already the lines are overgrown with weeds, despite freight trains still regularly using the line.

Although closed completely for 33 years at the time of this visit, an oil tank wagon still remains in the siding. This is not as odd as it seems, as the wagon belongs to the Tenterden Railway Company and had not been accidentally left behind by BR. *Mike Esau/TG*

The 'South Eastern Limited', hauled by Class 'A1X' No 32662, approaches Bodiam on 11 June 1961. Coal was still delivered by rail at this time and is being loaded on to lorries in traditional sacks for local distribution.

Today the coal yard has closed and the way forward to Robertsbridge is blocked by dense undergrowth. It is unlikely that the Tenterden Railway Company will restore passenger services beyond here, at least in the foreseeable future. *Both TG*

Junction Road Halt

Less than a mile west of Bodiam the line crosses yet another road, this time the A229 from Maidstone to Hastings, near which Junction Road Halt was built as a private station and used by the public from about 1903. It was known as 'Junction Road for Hawkhurst', even in BR days. Special trains (other than for hop-pickers) rarely stopped here, although on 12 April 1958 one such did; as normal there was one engine on each end, the propelling engine being Class 'A1X' No 32636.

The second view shows the abandoned halt and track following the withdrawal of services. The buildings on the right are part of a hop farm, the main reason for the survival of the station for so long.

There is no trace of the railway viewed from the same point in the summer of 1996. A railway '10mph' speed restriction sign has, however, been erected by the adjacent private road. The halt was situated in the left foreground. *Mrs H. Sykes, courtesy of The Colonel Stephens Railway Museum/Lens of Sutton/TG*

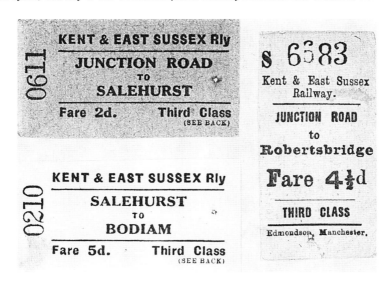

KESR bus-style tickets for issuing on the train.

Salehurst Halt

The only intermediate station on the KESR not situated by a road crossing was Salehurst Halt. It also had the distinction of being one of the few stations located close to the village it claimed to serve. The boarded crossing carried a public footpath from the village; there was no vehicular access.

By the summer of 1996 the trackbed had become completely overwhelmed by vegetation and almost all trace of the platform has gone, although the footpath still passes over the old trackbed. *Mike Esau/TG*

The tradition of a 'Terrier' at each end is maintained in this view of another special passing the hopfields near Salehurst Halt in the 1950s. The 'present view' shows the same location from a slightly greater distance, with hopfields still in evidence. The course of the railway follows the hedge-line in the middle distance. *Mike Esau/TG*

Robertsbridge

This is the crossing over the A21 main road from Tonbridge to Hastings, about half a mile from Robertsbridge. This location is named Northbridge Street and immediately to the right is a flour mill, served by a siding that also crossed the main road. The triangular structure beyond the crossing gate is the remains of a wind pump used to supply water to the railway.

A visit in the summer of 1996 found several remains of the railway including the level crossing gate posts and the base of the wind pump. The road is no longer the A21, as Robertsbridge now has a by-pass that carries this number. *Mike Esau/TG*

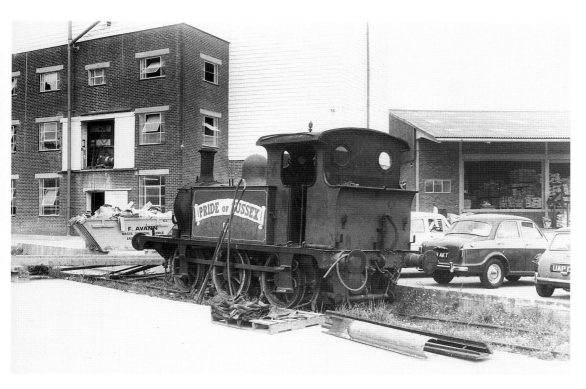

The mill continued to have deliveries by rail after closure of the KESR in 1961, and operated the remnant of the line as a siding from Robertsbridge, using its own locomotive. Class 'P' No 31556 was purchased from BR for this purpose, and named *Pride of Sussex*. It is seen here in 1970 just after the siding closed. Shortly afterwards it was acquired by the Tenterden Railway Company and renumbered 11. It has recently been repainted in SR green livery and given its former SR number of 1556. This engine was the first to be hired by the KESR from the SR in 1936.

The mill is still open, although under different ownership. The buildings have been altered a little, but the same location is easily recognisable. *Both TG*

The KESR met the SECR line from London to Hastings at the north end of Robertsbridge station. On 11 June 1961 Class 'A1X' No 32670 shunts the 'South Eastern Limited' stock round the curve of the KESR line. This was the last train to run to Tenterden Town under BR ownership.

A visit on 5 August 1995 found that the platforms had been lengthened and the main line electrified, but surprisingly the track into the old KESR bay is still in place. *Both TG*

Before track was removed in the Robertsbridge area, stock for the Tenterden Railway was transferred by rail. Here an 0-4-0 well tank named *The King* and the Ford Motor Company's diesel locomotive (see page 48) await removal to Tenterden. The latter was acquired in 1966 and the following year was loaned to the mill. It made its way to Tenterden in 1972. The well tank left the Tenterden Railway before its re-opening and is currently at the Fleetwood Locomotive Centre.

A down parcels train hauled by electro-diesel Class '73' No 73133 passes the same point on 8 August 1989, by which time the old KESR connection had been relaid with concrete sleepers. *Both TG*

Classes 'D1' No 31749 and 'L1' No 31786 stand in the KESR bay on 11 June 1961, waiting to take over the 'South Eastern Limited'. On the right is six-coach DMU No 1006 of Class 6S (201). These units were built at Eastleigh specially for the London to Hastings services, where narrow-bodied stock was mandatory by virtue of small tunnel bores. Similar vehicles of this class have been preserved and are marshalled as No 1001, which worked on the Tenterden Railway during 1995. The second photograph shows the special leaving Robertsbridge for London on the same evening. *Both TG*

The two 'Terriers' that worked the special over the KESR, Nos 32670 and 32662, stand on the main line at Robertsbridge. The KESR bay is occupied by an engineers train consisting of several BR 'Grampus' ballast wagons and an SR brake-van.

The 16.40 Charing Cross to Hastings train stands in the same platform on 5 August 1995, with 4-CEP EMU (Class 411) No 1541 on the rear. Narrow-bodied stock is no longer necessary, as there is single track through the tunnels. *Both TG*

A freight train from the KESR is seen on the down main line at Robertsbridge on 1 May 1958. The engine is No 32636. The second view of the same platform shows two Class 'L' 4-4-0s, Nos 31760 and 31768, bringing a special train from London into Robertsbridge on 18 October 1959. The stock was transferred to the KESR and taken to Tenterden by two 'Terriers'.

In the third photograph the 'South Eastern Limited' is arriving at Robertsbridge with Class 'H' No 31308 on the front. A tank engine at the head of such a long train is unusual, but this and the 4-4-0 behind were chosen to represent typical motive power in Kent in commemoration of the end of steam in the county.

Finally, 4-CIG EMU (Class 421) No 1813 forms an afternoon Charing Cross to Hastings train in August 1995. The footbridge across the main line has been renewed and relocated a few yards further south. *K. A. Stone, courtesy of The Colonel Stephens Railway Museum/TG (3)*

The Brighton Works shunter, Class 'A1X' No DS377, in the KESR bay at Robertsbridge on 19 October 1958, waiting to take its special train to Tenterden Town. Passengers transferred to this train from a special from London, the stock of which is to the right. The 'present' view shows the abandoned bay in 1996. *Both TG*

Left A special ticket issued by BR Western Region in conjunction with the 'Rother Valley Limited'.

2nd - SPECIAL ARRANGEMENT
OCTOBER 19th, 1958.
LOCOMOTIVE CLUB of GREAT BRITAIN
"THE ROTHER VALLEY LIMITED"
EXCURSION

Paddington to Herne Hill, Oxted, Tonbridge,
Robertsbridge, Tenterden, Bexhill(West).
Crowhurst, Hastings, Newhaven Harbour
and Victoria

(W) (6764)

For conditions see over

260

260

A mixed train from Tenterden Town hauled by No 32678 stands in the KESR bay on 7 August 1951. There is plenty of goods activity with coal in the yard and milk churns on the platform.

No 32678 is also the subject of the second photograph, this time fulfilling a very different role on 19 October 1958. The engine is attached to the rear of the 'Rother Valley Limited' and will propel the train to Tenterden Town. The special was run to commemorate the replacement of steam by diesel traction on both the KESR and Hastings main line.

Looking north along the abandoned bay in 1996, the yard is now occupied by bins for recycling purposes, although there is still some track on the extreme right-hand side, which is occupied by the headquarters of the Rother Valley Railway group, whose objective is to restore the KESR line in the Robertsbridge area. *A. J. Pike, courtesy of Frank Hornby/TG (2)*

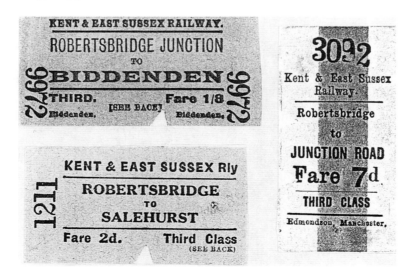

On 26 April 1947 the 9.48am from Rolvenden behind engine No 3 stands unusually in the main-line platform at Robertsbridge. A little earlier in the morning, but nearly 50 years later, 4-VEP EMU (Class 423) No 3573 enters the station on a Charing Cross to Hastings train. *H. C. Casserley/TG*

A more general view of Robertsbridge from the south end of the station on the same day in 1947. The Rolvenden train can be seen at the down platform and passengers on the up side are waiting for the train to Charing Cross. Note that the station nameboard refers to the KESR line.

On 5 June 1996 a train from Hastings stops at Robertsbridge to collect a good number of passengers for London. This is a well-used station and many people commute from here to London. There is an hourly service throughout the day, with extra trains at peak periods. The rear unit is 4-VEP EMU No 3511. *H. C. Casserley/TG*

INDEX

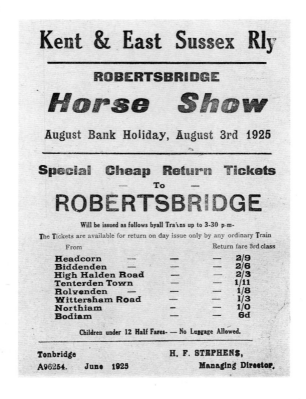